Millenial Trash

By Duckie May

They poured sludge into the water
And burned fire through the woods
They dug deep into her soul
And raped her of all her goods
They cut down all the trees
And uprooted every plant
They slaughtered every bison
And defaced the elephants
Their smoke billowed into the air
From their machines and cigarettes
They threw plastic into the rivers
Without thought or any regret
They took all they could take
And then took a little more
Until there was nothing left
They had won the great war
But all that was around them
Were remnants left and ash
Melted ice filled the oceans full
And their huge mountains of trash
So she swallowed them all whole
With high winds and floods of rain
And she started all over
But without them again

Minimum wage 50 hours a week
Today is painful, the future is bleak
My useless degree sits in a box
While I work away under the clock
Depression is fierce and nothing's secure
My glasses are weak and I'm uninsured
The world is dying and we are to blame
My back hurts and my joints are inflamed
I vape away and drown my sorrows
In weed and alcohol and money I borrow
I need soap and my cabinets are bare
My rent is late and I'm so scared
I have no meds and my car needs fuel
My kids risk their lives going to school
A dictator in power and Nazis with guns
I can't believe what we've all become
I've always wanted to be an adult
But this really wasn't the intended result
I'm miserable more as the days pass by
I wish I weren't here so I wait to die
They say I am spoiled and it's all my fault
That my car loan and mortgage are in default
But they don't understand what it means to live
Drowning in a world that won't forgive

Come with me my love,
Follow me to the stars
We will fly above
The night sky is ours
Close your eyes my love
Feel the wind on your face
And we'll go high enough
And reach outer space
The night is alive my love
Reach for the moon
And touch the sky because
It will end too soon
Dance with me my love
While we still can
In the sky above
Just give me your hand

Waking up to another day
Waking up to feeling this way
It haunts the shadows and the halls
It creeps the dusk as night falls
This feeling of dread that won't go away
This feeling of pain and great dismay
I've cried all my tears, a river of grief
Feeling the fear with no relief
The waves crash in and bring me down
They crash again, I start to drown
This darkness haunts me day and night
The darkness taunts me all my life
I wish it would end so I could breathe
But it carries on with no reprieve
The depression lingers, so unwanted
To the tips of my fingers, forever haunted

Hey hun it's me, your old school friend
I have an offer that I wish to extend
Want to lose the weight that I see you have gained?
I know it's been years but let me explain
I have oils on sale, two for one
I have wraps and creams and shakes too hun!
Throw out your meds, I have the fix
Just try this mineral vegan mix
I want to help you live your very best life
So see what I have and heed my advice
Try my pills and vitamins and CBD too
I have all these things on sale for you!
I can change your life for $19.99
Just try all these products of mine
I can fix you and make you happy and thin
But wait, what is your name again?

Covered in crystals, the scent is strong
Break a bud and get out the bong
Grind it up and roll a fatty
Light it up, that wacky tobacc-y
Deep inhale and hold it in
Slow exhale and do it again!
Puff puff pass, to your right
Breathe it in, that green delight
Don't bogart the piece to tell a story
Puff puff pass all the green glory
Wait till it hits you, it's a creeper
You will feel alive and think deeper
So many ideas, laughter and smoke
Breathe it all in and take a toke
That wacky tobacc-y sure hits the spot
And sometimes in life, it's all that I got

Rise and shine, vitals at five
Here at the psych ward, you know you're alive
Blue slipper socks and pills in a cup
All to make the voices shut-up
No strings or laces, no coffee or weed
Meds help the paranoid delusions believed
The food is awful, try to keep it down
Just wait for the doctor to make his rounds
Read an old book or play a card game
All to pass time, every day is the same
We are all waiting and want to go home
So we call family on the patient's phone
Visiting hours are at four, lights out at ten
The beds are hard and the blankets are thin
The psych ward is cold, hard and stiff
And it is home and family that we miss
So we wait until it is our turn to leave
And they call our name for our release

I'm out of weed again, there is no more
There is no green gold that I adore
My bag is empty, my jar is too
And my guy is out of what he grew
I want some bud to calm me down
Before I have a full meltdown
I pace the house and the hall
and wait for a text or a call
It's so hard to have none
This really isn't any fun
Once he gets it, he will text
And I know what will happen next
He will say he is on his way
And for hours I will wait

I love the smell of the brew
The joe in my cup
I love all that has to do
And all it's made of
It pours hot from the pot
And into my mug
I sip it because it's hot
Like a warm hug
I drink away and get some more
Of that liquid black gold
I fill my cup as it pours
It will never get old
But the pot grows empty too
And I have to refill
So I fill it up and make some new
Until the pot is filled
My morning coffee is so pure
Of energy and life
So I add milk and sugar and stir
To make the morning bright
I've got to have my joe
My liquid best friend
Because I love it so
My special coffee blend

Way back when, a simpler time
When I was about 8 or 9
I had no worries or any care
I had food to eat and clothes to wear
No job except take out the trash
Do your homework and take a bath
Why can't I go back to those days
When all I did was run and play
But now I live at a dead end
And I'm all alone and have no friends
I wish I could go back to the past
And visit the times that have passed
I want to be a kid again
To run and play with my friends
But instead I am growing old and grey
And time passes by day by day
Oh I wish that I could go back to when
I was a child so I could laugh again

Maybe it took years
Or you knew right away
Maybe you're trans
Or maybe you're gay
You thought you were weird
And something was broken
But really you're queer
The truth has been spoken
There are others like you
And you aren't alone
You are so loved
Your truth is your own
You are just perfect
From head to toe
You're easy to love
And I thought you should know ❤

Khaki shorts and socks with sandals
This boomer is too hot to handle
A MAGA hat and Stars and Stripes
He's never wrong and always right
He waters his lawn twice a day
He never tips and always complains
There's a virus on his computer again
He loves Fox News and hates CNN
"Entitled brats" he shouts from his pension
And his untaxed income he failed to mention
He litters freely without guilt or concern
And he doesn't care if the world burns
Science is a fraud and he is the king
He knows it all and wants everything
Salute the flag and pray to Jesus
Save no one except a fetus
Follow the laws when it is convenient
And say that the world is too lenient
Whip the kids to teach them a lesson
And argue today's parental progression
He's a grumpy old man with no sympathy
He doesn't care and has no empathy
This boomer stands for all that is wrong
And what we've fought for all along
Oh he's a man's man, one of the guys
He bottles his emotions and never cries
But the part that makes me the most sad
Is this boomer isn't nobody; it's my dad

I don't wanna get out of bed today
I don't wanna think
I didn't sleep at all last night
Not even a wink
This sadness keeps me down all day
Hiding in my bed
My worries keep me up all night
The thoughts in my head
I don't wanna be here today
Not even alive
So I battle my thoughts and fight
Trying to survive
I woke up to another day
I wish wasn't so
And nothing seems to be alright
And I feel so low
I don't wanna be alive today
I don't wanna go on
But I guess I'll stay another night
And another dawn
I know there will be better days
And I will be free
So I will put up a fight
In my misery
I don't wanna be here today
But I will defend
My right to a better life
Until the bitter end

It's payday again, I got the deposit
I wanted a coffee so I splurged and bought it
Time to pay the car note and the phone bill again
And payback the money I borrowed from a friend
Two hundred in overdrafts and a returned check
fee
Send cash, a money order or pay directly
Put gas in the car and pay the insurance
And lean on a friend for reassurance
Because the bills are paid and now I am broke
This is turning into a really sick joke
Not a dime to my name and behind on my bills
And worried thoughts from the anxiety I feel
The cabinets are bare and I need my meds
But I can't do much with an account in red
Maybe I shouldn't have bought that coffee today
Because now I'm out of money on this pay day

We have joined the others
In the drop off line
The fathers and mothers
Rise and shine
Take off your belt
And grab your bag
Knees to chest
Do not lag
I'll slow to a crawl
So open the door
I won't stop at all
Just a second more
It's almost our turn
So hit the ground running
Get ready to learn
No time for hugging
No long speeches
Tuck and roll
Storm the beaches
Now go go go!

I have a thought that I wish to share
And I'm gonna use confession bear
I'll get some upvotes and maybe some likes
When I share it on reddit tonight
It's kinda funny but totally true
You will probably relate to it too
I'll post a gif of my face when
And share the unpopular puffin
Ermahgerd will get some laughs
And I will complain on grumpy cat
Scumbag Steve will be a jerk
And I'll post a gif of Tina's twerk
I'll take advice from a duck
And laugh at all of Brian's luck
Top text or bottom, you'll know what I mean
When I share how I feel on a dank meme
It's an inside joke between everyone
It's really insightful and so much fun
So get ready to see what I have to say
In a meme on the Internet today

There's something I want to tell you
I need you to listen
There's something about me
That's always been different
My whole life I've been this way
This isn't new
But I know who I am now
I know my truth
I've never felt like a boy
But I've never felt like a girl
I don't feel like a woman
I feel like something more
I've learned there is a name for it
And that I'm not alone
I've discovered I'm non-binary
I've found my home
Please use they or them
I'm not a she
This is really important
Please listen to me
It may not make sense
And it doesn't have to
But this is who I am
And I need to tell you
I am not a boy or a girl
I'm in between
I'm something more

And now you know me
Capitalism kills
But they don't tell you that
They say it is the freedom
That's being attacked
Work will set you free
They shout from their towers
As we fight for scraps
And they wave their powers
One dollar to vote
And three to eat
Another to breathe
And live on the street
We work to live
For our right to exist
We won't live to work
Under a Marxist
It's all for profit
Even if it kills
Work yourself to death
Just to pay the bills
Don't you feel free
With so many colors?
So much to buy
And so many others
Don't you feel free
Tonight after work
Twelve hours a day
Just like clockwork
Maybe when you are old
You will get to rest
But now you work to live
And try your best
No profit for your labor

And all that you do
Just minimum wages
Is all that you're due
Work yourself to death
Sunup to sun down
Get no respect
And slowly drown
You'll be replaced
By tomorrow afternoon
So keep working away
Or else you're doomed

Day two of no smokes
It's been a ride
And I've tried to quit
A hundred times
Closer to death
Ten dollars a pack
And the slow suicide
Of a heart attack
I stink like ashes
My fingers are stained
My lungs are burning
And my voice is strained
So I've got to do this
I owe it to myself
I've got to quit smoking
And do it for my health
I have to learn
To live without smokes
No crutch to lean on
To find my hope
They got me good
And I'm addicted
So I've got to live
Without the wicked
No more smokes
No more fags
I mean it for good

But just one more drag

It's going so fast
my mind is racing
I can't hold still
or stop pacing
It's 1 am
and I should be sleeping
But instead
my soul is weeping
I write it out
on blank paper
And I become
the story maker
The words come fast
and I submit
To the stories
at my fingertips
It flows like water
the twists of the plot
And all the stories
from my thoughts
It's painful to write
uncomfortable to say
But the truth is
I like it that way
My mind is chaos
and it moves quick
It's how I write
it's my trick
All of my passion
or none at all
I don't know how
to balance it all
My mind is chaos
but I write
Instead of sleeping

Back in the days of Britney
And 98 degrees
Back when we had Whitney
And lived carefree
We smelled like cucumber melons
And glitter lip gloss
We were only ten or eleven
When time was lost
The slow jams of N*SYNC
played at the dance
And we would all lip sync
If given the chance
No bills, just homework
And tidy your room
F•R•I•E•N•D•S at Central Perk
And in the classroom
I miss the days of freedom
It went too fast
And now I really need some
And I'm busting my ass
Let's go back to the good days
When all we had to do
Was eat and learn and play
That was all that we knew
Go back to the tamagotchi
And Blues Clues
Back to when my mom bought me
Clear jelly shoes
I miss the little things

From way back when
Like playing The Sims
And gel pens
Those days are gone now
And it's reality
I'm an adult now
And I'm no longer free

Did I say something weird?
I feel like I did
I've had this really big fear
Since I was a kid
This fear of socializing
It's just too much
My habit of over-analyzing
And the stress of such
Did I embarrass myself
Or act a fool
Did I fail as well
As act like a tool
This anxiety is painful
I hate it so
And I'm not able
To make it go
I stress over it all
Every last word
My confidence will fall
And I'll go unheard
This anxiety is exhausting
I want to relax
This is all costing
My strength to lapse
I'm just gonna go home
And away from this
Don't call on the phone
I will dismiss
I am such a loser

Broken to pieces
I fear the future
When the anxiety releases
Stop talking to me
I can't take it
Just let me be
Because I can't fake it

I listened to your music all the time
Back when you were in your prime
I have your movies and posters too
But something is bothersome about you
I read your words that were so mean
And you aren't as nice as you seem
Say goodbye to your fans and yours truly
Because all that you are is a bully
Your racist remarks have left a stain
And now you're losing all your fame
You're cancelled and your career is dead
From the racist remarks that you said
I'm deleting your songs and losing interest
And now your career is truly finished
Maybe you would still have some fans
If you weren't a bigot that got banned

Spare the rod and spoil the child
They say that's why the kids are wild
They say to beat them into submission
But they don't care about the cognition
They demand respect but give none
When they spank their kids on the bum
Some may have autism or adhd
But instead they turn them over their knee
They learn fear and pain from their parents
And all it does is leave them embarrassed
Learn to parent your kids without pain
Because your lazy parenting is to blame
The kids learn nothing except to be afraid
And that's not how kids should be raised
Hurting your kids is a really bad move
And you act like you've got something to prove
All you're doing is breaking their heart
And teaching them violence when things fall apart

I was five when I had my first crush
And he kissed my cheek on the school bus
But as I grew older I saw my attraction
Wasn't all to boys, but a fraction
The other half of me liked girls too
And non-binary people are also cool
I like them all and gender is irrelevant
Men are hot and women are elegant
Pixie cuts drive me completely wild
And men with a beard get me all riled
Being bisexual is so much fun
Because I am attracted to everyone!

I posted my thoughts in a tweet
And shared a meme on my newsfeed
Instagram has all of my pics
And my page is high traffic
I crack a joke on a status
And react to a post that's the saddest
I share a link on my timeline
And share a quote from Einstein
I get my news from frontpage reddit
And to share a picture I will embed it
My aunt in Utah says hello
I'll add some people I barely know
I'll tell you what I'm having for dinner
And I'll send a DM to my sister
I love to socialize from behind a screen
And tag a friend so my post is seen
I'll attach a gif for my face when
And a shoutout to all of my friends
Social media is so great
To socialize with your mates

I didn't plan for this
I thought I would be dead
I'm 32 and it's
that I didn't plan ahead
I thought I'd die someway
Probably by my own hand
But I'm still here today
This isn't what I planned
So I have this career that's dead
And no education to share
And tomorrow I will dread
The days of nowhere
My life is a disaster now
I wish I had the skills
To make a difference somehow
And pay off all my bills
I don't know what tomorrow holds
I thought I would be gone
But the days unfold
Into another dawn
I planned to kill myself
Before I became a grown up
I thought I'd bid farewell
I didn't think I'd grow up
But I'm here right now
Doing my thing
But I'm curious now
Of what tomorrow brings

So I'll stick around
Just a little bit more
I'm not in the ground
Or a child anymore
I didn't plan for this
I thought I would be dead
But look at what I would miss
And all that's ahead
I'm gonna keep going on
And get through today
I'll keep chugging along
And onto another day

They say we ruined the industry
Of golf and hotels
But it is because we live differently
And we aren't doing well
We can't afford to dine out
So we cook at home
Not to mention the fall out
Of the landline phone
We stopped shopping at the mall
Because we are too poor
They blame it on the fall
Of our loyalty and more
We skip church and Jesus
And play frisbee golf instead
And all for the reasons
That religion is dead
We don't want diamonds
Or cable television
Our job is dead end
And our degrees are useless
Communism we contend
And we cut off the abusive
But we are bringing back houseplants
And facial hair
And sometimes we square dance
And barter and share
We embrace mental health

And spread kindness
But we have no wealth
To buy the finest
We focus on what's important
Like happiness and love
Instead of the boring
Status quo thereof
Our lives are different
Than the other generations
But it's significant
That we've cancelled discrimination
We aim to kill racism dead
So we punch the nazis cold
And we love instead
Of following the old
Our generation is killing industries
Like knocking on the door
But it's because we can't have luxuries
On our income of poor
So we make do with what we have
And upcycle what we can
We cut consumption in half
And respect other humans
We bring peace and respect
Instead of shopping bags
It's not about the objects
But the love that we have
But we worry about the climate
And end circumcision
We can't buy a house

So all we do is rent
And we don't marry our spouse
Even if we are content
We won't reproduce
Because the world is dying
And we buy fresh produce
Instead of boxed meals dining
We can't afford to live
The way of our parents
So we can'tIn the life we inherit
No honeymoons or breakfast
We do intermittent fasting
And we run for the exit
Of the industries crashing
We skip the luxuries
Because we can't afford it
And we have enough worries
And we can't ignore it have kids

You say that you're a feminist
But I have to disagree
Because you are supremacist
To a certain degree
You exclude who you want
And only accept who fits
Because you are nonchalant
And their struggles you dismiss
Black women need support
But you only care about yourself
And you really fall short
And you're mean as hell
You fight with a pussy hat
And chant the songs
But that's not where it's at
You've got it all wrong
You exclude who you want
Whatever fits your agenda
Sex workers you will taunt
And all the other genders
Stop thinking about you
Just for a minute
Because all that you do
Is so you can win it
Feminism is for everyone
No excluding people
Because we are all someone
Who wants to be equal
Use your voice to amplify
The struggle of the others
Don't be a bad guy
Let's help one another

I am an adult now
So I do what I please
I can do what I want now
I have me to appease
Crackers in bed
And a snack before dinner
I'll have ice cream instead
And all of the liquor
I'll sleep until noon
And not wear my pants
I won't clean my room
Or plan in advance
You can't make me obey
Because I am an adult now
And I like it this way
I choose what I allow
I used to hold back
And follow the rules
But now I attack
And skip school
Juice box in my lunch
And cartoons on tv
Cake for brunch
No vegetables for me
I'm an adult now
I do what I desire
And I know now
What I didn't know prior
I'm just a big kid
Watching cartoons
And you can't forbid
Anything that I do

It started when I was young
And looking in the mirror
I hated what I saw
And it became clearer
I hated my stomach
And all of my thighs
Compared to the tv
And the media lies
My stretch marks are shameful
And my breasts are too small
And I am not able
To change it at all
Their skin is so perfect
Mine is blotchy and red
And it isn't worth it
I'm better off dead
Why am I so ugly
With a funny nose
I'm just a mess
And trash I suppose
I wish I was thinner
And had a nice butt
But my feet are ugly
And my pudgy gut
I feel so hideous
Compared to you all
Why am I so ugly
And so very tall
I hate my body
Every inch and wrinkle
From head to toe
And my skin dimples
But I can't do anything
To change how I look
So instead I will focus

On a positive outlook
You seemed ok at first
When we first met
But what you have endorsed
Is making me fret
Your kids are running around
Without protection
And you seem so proud
Of their infection
No vaccines you said
"They are dangerous."
But you will kill them dead
And endanger us
Measles and mumps
Are preventable
And chickenpox bumps
Are dangerous medical
But instead you refrain
And make up excuses
In your stupid brain
And it's honestly abusive
And I just find it funny
When you smoke your cigarettes
And say it's about money
And you have no regrets
So when your sick child
Infects a new baby
It won't be mild
You stupid lady
Vaccinate your kids dumbass
It's not about you
It's for the others dumbass
Who will die from the flu

I have Netflix and Hulu and Amazon Prime
And that's how I spend a lot of my time
Binge watching shows, one after another
There are so many shows that I will discover
Old flicks and new, horror and drama
To enjoy while I lay around in my pajamas
There's a new season out, I'll binge tonight
And I'll laugh at all the jokes that they write
My favorite is Orange Is The New Black
And I'll watch episodes back to back
Funniest Videos makes me laugh
As I watch the old videos from the past
Movies galore and documentaries
And I will recite the lines from memory
I'll hide in my room away from the world
While I watch shows like Boy Meets World
Facebook Watch has videos too
And to the screen I will be glued
But the truth is I'm hiding from reality
While I sit and binge watch the TV
My world is so depressing and very boring
So I spend my time on the TV exploring
I'm hiding in the shows to cover my pain
Because all the comedy distracts my brain
So I binge watch the shows to pass time

On Netflix and Hulu and Amazon Prime

My heart is racing
And I am pacing
The stress I'm facing
Has me bracing
Heart palpitations
With no explanations
This stressful situation
Has me in fixation
My mind is spinning
My patience are thinning
This is the beginning
I can't stop thinking
It's driving me mad
The stress I have
It's so very bad
The worst I've had
I'm going to breathe
While I seethe
And grit my teeth
From the stress underneath
I can't take this anymore
My heart is sore
And my feelings roar
Like never before
I pace the hall
While I bawl
As my skin crawls
From the stress of it all
This stress is so much
My heart is crushed
I'm stressed as such
From anxiety's touch
But I count to ten
And breathe it in
And I try again

To calm and grin

You don't see the pain I'm in
Or recognize my struggle
The hurt is beneath my skin
And so very subtle
You see an able body
And I have a battle
And you see nobody
But I tread and paddle
It's not on my face
Or out for you to view
It's not all over the place
Or on display for you
The pain hides away
And I will carry on
And it hurts today
The pain is never gone
My struggle is hidden beneath
My skin where I hide
And I struggle to keep
My pain deep inside
You see an able body
And I am not fully well
And not everybody

Has a disability you can tell
You say you're a man
A really nice guy
You're so much nicer than
All the other guys
Your tough thick skin
Makes it easy to say
A joke that's been
On my mind today
You're so level headed
And never grow upset
And never get offended
By a joke or protest
So I tell a joke to laugh
At your demeanor and life
A joke on your behalf
A joke that applies
We will just laugh along
At your silliness and then
How you were wrong
And stupid you've been
I know you will get it
And not grow upset
You won't throw a fit
Or yell a threat
Mr. Man's man
Mr. Tough guy
You are so much more than
A man who cries
So just listen to my joke
At your expense
My little poke
At your offense
Laugh along sir
You're so rational
You're so much stronger

And it's so laughable

I breathe in smoke
As I take a toke
Oh that sweet indica
It fills my lungs
Over my tongue
Oh that sweet indica
I exhale slow
I watch it glow
Oh that sweet indica
My body rests
As I take a breath
Oh that sweet indica
My mind slows down
Friends are around
Oh that sweet indica
I pass to the left
And I start to drift
Oh that sweet indica
This smoke is sweet
Fuzzy from head to feet
Oh that sweet indica

They hired me at minimum wage
Bachelor's degree required
Now they've got me at this stage
And I fear I will be fired
I work away for pennies now
Just trying to survive
But I can't pay my bills anyhow
What a waste of a life
They make dollars from my labor
My boss and the company
I work away in my chamber
And I'm watched distrustfully
I have no future or soul left
I'm just an empty shell
And I am always so stressed
In this office work hell
But dying is my fear
And having nowhere to go
So I work for years
With nothing to show
I have to eat tonight
And I will keep going
So I'll be alright
With this fear of not knowing
I'm gonna keep working along
Until I stop drowning
But the work is long
And I'm constantly doubting
I wish I could take a break
And afford to live
But instead I make mistakes
And give and give
One day I'll have enough
And I will just relax
One day all this working stuff

Will be in the past
You ask "How are you?"
While standing on my porch
But no details, I will spare you
You don't know what you're in for
I didn't sleep at all last night
I'm out of my meds
And the day has been a fight
With an ache in my head
I am nodding off as time passes
And I can't make a meal
I've misplaced my reading glasses
But it's not a big deal
I won't tell you my bad thoughts
The ones that drive me crazy
Or the nonsense that I've bought
Or what I've been doing lately
I know you expect me to respond
With a smile and an okay
So I will tell you I'm fine because
You really don't care today
Your inquiry is just a reflex
There is no care for the answer
And the lingering effects
Of the truth of what's the matter
So "I'm doing okay today."
"And how are you?" I'll ask
You'll think I am fine this way
And I'll hide behind my mask

The weight of the world hits me
Before I open my eyes
Death again missed me
It's not a surprise
I thought I was done last night
When I went to bed
But a new day has come overnight
And I wish I were dead
A new day is here today
What I don't want
I wish death would come someday
It's always a taunt
When I go to sleep I pray
That it will end
But I woke up again today
It's a trend
I don't want to go on anymore
To live this life
Because I can't battle much more
In this fight
Every day I wish to be numb
Until the end
But every day I succumb
When it begins

I'm out of coffee
and soda too
But I gotta wait
and make do
My car needs gas
And I need smokes
But payday is Friday
And I'm so broke
Gotta make a meal
Out of the pantry
Some leftover stew
Nothing too fancy
Ration the toilet paper
Wash clothes in the tub
Pawn off a necklace
To get food because
Payday is in three days
And I need money
My light bill is due
And my cats are hungry
We gotta make do
With what we got
While we wait for Friday
In this tight spot

I open my mouth
To swallow them south
A handful of meds
Right before bed
A swig from a cup
To keep my chin up
One for peace
Another for relief
One for the voices
And better choices
One for sleep
And for upkeep
These meds of mine
Are the best of times
They keep me stable
Alive and able

If I had to go back
And do it all again
I would do the same
From beginning to end
All the love I lost
And the heartache received
Was leading up to you
And the love we've conceived
All the wrong turns
Were in the right direction
All the mistakes
Lead up to your affection
My past prepared me
For a lifetime of love
And I made it out barely
For your kisses and hugs
I now know love
It is so true
And the things of my past
Prepared me for you

I should have said no
Like I felt in my gut
Instead I said go
No matter what
I had gotten my dress
Pearls and shoes
I was so stressed
Of what to do
But the guests arrived
The photographer too
And at a quarter past five
We said "I do"
But four years later
And two babies in
We lived in anger
From the pain within
But one day I woke up
And saw the destruction
And I picked my chin up
To begin the construction
I went out on my own
To a new life and things
I made my own home
And spread my wings

Swing a hammer and change a tire
These are things that are required
They say a man must never cry
Or be a soft emotional guy
Always tough and never forgiving
Never gives up and always winning
But I'm here to say that men can feel
They can live out loud and not conceal
They love to cuddle and hug too
Flowers delivered and I Love You's
A man's heart is soft and full of love
With gentle hands beneath his gloves
A true man sticks to his word
And speaks up for those not heard
Let's raise our boys to be better men
Better dads, husbands and friends

Unfold socks and untuck sleeves
Toss them in the big machine
Add some soap and watch them spin
Then they'll wash and rinse again
Stain removal with some Shout
And in the dryer to air them out
Switch the loads and start another
Match the socks to each other
Stack the pants and hang the shirts
Iron the dresses and fold the skirts
It keeps stacking and never stops
Washing the laundry and folding the socks
The hamper is empty and we're all done
This laundry day is not much fun

I like your pics and I heart react
I love it when you make me laugh
Your aesthetic is always so stunning
I love it when your cameras are running
I've been following you for a while
I love your life and your style
So I was wondering what you thought
About me and these feelings I've caught
I'm single now and you are too
So I've been wanting to DM you
I know we live oceans apart
But I have to tell you what's in my heart
We can text or call on the phone
And connect through the time zones
I'll get on a plane to see your face
Or you can even come to my place
I'll take you out on the town
And take a walk to show you around
Maybe you are my soulmate
And this is all falling from fate
But I wanted to see what you thought
If we get together and give it a shot

Women and them's of femme delight
All join together to put up a fight
Black women bleed for justice coming
For the men and sons of those becoming
The disabled fight for equal access too
For an equal opportunity in all they do
We fight for our right to have an abortion
And our right to be a feminine person
Equal pay and daycare would change lives
For all of the daughters, sisters and wives
Feminism's song is sung for the femmes
For all of our family and all of our friends
And when she sings her songs in the night
That's when we come and join the fight

When we laugh out loud, we "lol"
And "wth" for what the hell
☺ is a smiley face
And sometimes we type in boldface
Online talk is all shorthand
With exclamation points and ampersands
"Lmfao" to laugh hysterically
Or just "haha" to laugh generically
A shrug emoji to show our indifference
Or share a ❤ for significance
wE tYpE LiKe tHiS foR SaRcASm
And use !! for enthusiasm
"omg" for oh my god
And clapping hands to applaud
Use ☹ to be super sad
And >:-(to be really mad
Send a text or a tweet
Say it now and don't delete
Share how you feel, it's so much fun
Online shorthand is for everyone!

"Sit like a lady," they said
As if my legs had something to hide
But I'm not a lady instead
So I spread my legs wide
"Curl your hair," they said
And put powder on your nose.
But I would rather die, I said
Or be a boy I suppose
"Wear a bra," they said
And high heel shoes
But I'll wear boots instead
And forget the rouge
"Talk like a lady," they said.
And be nice to the men
But I'll talk to the ladies instead
And fall in love with them

Available at
amazon.com/author/duckiemay